The XIT Ranch
How Texas Traded Land For a State House

By Anne Haw Holt

Copyright 2017 by A. H. Holt
All rights reserved, including the right to
reproduce this book,
or portions thereof, in any form.

ISBN-10:0-9983877-0-3
ISBN-13:978-0-9983877-0-3

Published by Old Atlanta Publishing LLC
oldatlantapublishing.com

Edited by Mark Sherfy

First Edition: March 2017

Printed in the United States of America

The XIT Ranch

Other Books By
A. H. Holt

Fiction

High Plains Fort
Ten in Texas
Silver Creek
Blanco Sol
Riding Fence
Kendrick
Blood Redemption

Nonfiction

Grant Writing Step by Step
From Writer to Author
Beautiful Places:
Monticello & Jefferson County Florida

Author's Note:

This paper was the inspiration for my novel TEN IN TEXAS. I have included here a copy of my first chapter showing you through the eyes of my hero Will Gantry, crowds of "land seekers" arriving in north Texas by train, ready to plow into farms small pieces of the great XIT Ranch.

A.H.Holt

The XIT Ranch
How Texas Traded Land For a State House

The acquisition of three million acres of rangeland in the Panhandle, the construction of a state capitol building, and the creation of the XIT Ranch is a big, fantastic story that could only happen in Texas. Timing made the XIT possible. Spanish cattle, railroad building, technological and business innovation, settlers seeking a better life in the west after the Civil War, and the millions of acres of land owned by the state of Texas came together to create one of the largest ranches in the world.

Texas' first bid to international attention was made through land. As the most effective use of the soil by a limited population lay in the frontier pursuit of free grazing, it was natural for the early Texas economy to rely on moving the great herds of wild cattle north and east to markets in Sedalia and New Orleans.

A Spanish expedition came into the province to found a settlement in 1690. They brought cattle with them. The cattle had long bodies and long legs, mottled brown, black and white hides and nasty dispositions.

Some of these cattle forded the Rio Grande and escaped from the expedition into the wilds of Nueces River Country. By the time the East Texas Missions were abandoned in 1693, wild cattle were grazing throughout their range. Even today, the long horns and head of a Spanish cow are part of any image of Texas.

By 1836, nearly a century and a half after the first Spanish expedition into Texas, settlers from the United States won the country from Mexico and created a republic. Ten years later, Texas entered the Union, with the important agreement that the state should retain all public lands. The new state of Texas possessed vast millions of acres unmeasured by a surveyor's chain. Many of these prairie lands no settler had ever set foot on.

When Texas first became a state, its scattered and meager population lived in the east and south of the state, occupying only a small portion of the expanse of its land. Texas was unquestionably land poor, but, it was on that poverty that the Texas public school system was built and the state university system was founded. The state's generous homestead policy allowed large ranches to secure their holdings and the state capitol at Austin to be built.

By 1880, only fifteen years after the Civil War, immigration tamed eastern Texas. Families pushing into the area transformed range land into farms and forced the cattle industry to move westward onto the dry plains, beyond the ninetieth meridian. Railroad building spread west and south, opening up the country.

Technological innovations such as improved windmills, pumps, barbed wire and the telephone, created new possibilities, many undreamed of before the war. New management methods such as vertical and horizontal integration developed to answer the demands of larger businesses with management divorced from the individual owner. The whole country was booming.

Chicago was the gateway to the west, spawning businesses and money ready to take advantage of every opportunity. It was a syndicate of Chicago businessmen who saw the potential of northern Texas.

Business leaders and investors from the northeastern United States, England, and Europe rushed to take part in developing the great open ranges of the American west. Cattle became the investment "bubble" of the day. Anyone could buy a few cheap Texas cows, throw them on some open prairie and build a money-making ranch. So many hopeful millionaires began to raise cattle that over-stocking, over-grazing, and the resulting glut of beef on the market was inevitable.

At the peak of the "bubble," some Chicago businessmen who believed in the opportunity offered by ranching and in the future of American business responded to Texas' offer to trade land for a capitol building. Texas was growing too fast for its tax base to keep up. There was no money to build needed public buildings. The legislature controlled the state's public lands, and used them to bargain for the construction of the state capitol building in Austin.

Texas used its public lands to encourage settlement, provide educational buildings, improve transportation and in this case, filled its growing need for adequate state government buildings. On November 17, 1875, the Texas Constitutional Convention at Austin voted to set aside three million acres to provide for the construction of a capitol building. This resolution was made part of the constitution that was ratified by the people of Texas in February 1876.

The legislature waited until 1879 to appropriate the 3,050,000 acres and create a commission to survey the Capitol Reservation. This property was in the northwest corner of the Panhandle and covered most of ten counties.

The legislators who lived and worked "down in the skillet" knew little of the Panhandle when they earmarked this land for the capitol project. They heartily congratulated themselves for their skill in trading three million acres of "arid" land for a great building. The Panhandle was called Los Llanos Estacados, the Staked Plains. To the Mexicans it was an impediment to travel, but penetrable. To the pioneers from the east it was a part of the Great American Desert, unknown and feared.

An unauthenticated story tells of Spanish padres who came down from Santa Fe in 1734 "to establish a fort and mission" at San Saba. They are said to have placed stakes along the way, carefully topping them with buffalo skulls, that they might be seen at a distance and provide a guide out of the plains.

The distant, all but unusable land of the Panhandle seemed of little value to the Texas legislature. They wanted, believed they desperately needed a capitol building.

E. E. Myers of Detroit drew a plan for the Texas Capitol. The Capitol Board approved the plan in 1881. The old capitol burned that same year, increasing the urgency of completing a new building as quickly as possible. Only two contractors submitted bids to construct the building, and the contract was awarded to Mattheas Schell of Rock Island, Illinois. Schell posted a $250,000 bond in January 1882. He began preparing ground for the building in

February 1882, but construction did not start until January 1883. [1]

To finance the necessary material and labor costs, Schell assigned ownership of three-fourths of the contract to Taylor, Babcock, and Company of Chicago. Later that year, he assigned the remaining one-fourth to Abner Taylor of the same syndicate. Amos C. Babcock was a prominent Republican leader. John V. Farwell, part owner of Taylor, Babcock, and Company was Chicago's largest dry goods wholesaler, and his brother Charles B. Farwell was a congressman who had helped organize the Republican Party.

Abner Taylor was also politically inclined, but particularly well known as the primary contractor in the rebuilding of Chicago after the great fire. These men supervised the building of the capitol building, laying the corner stone in March 1885, and completing the work in April 1888. [2]

The estimated cost for construction of the capital was $1,500,000, but final material and labor costs to Taylor, Babcock, and Company were $3,224,593.45. The Texas legislature paid for the work with clear title to three million acres of grazing land, possibly the "biggest land swap in Texas history."

State officials turned the land over to Taylor, Babcock, and Company gradually, according to the company's progress in completing the building. Well-watered land in the Panhandle was then selling for $0.55 or less per acre, in parcels of at least one section (640 acres). The cost per acre would have been much less for a three-million-acre piece. Any land away from water was worth no more than $0.25 per acre. Therefore, Taylor, Babcock, and Company paid more than twice the value of the finest, well-watered land in the area for every acre of the three million acres they received for constructing the capitol. [3]

Cost over-runs on the project began with the stone Taylor, Babcock, and Company planned to use for construction of the building's walls. The Chicago syndicate obtained a right-of-way to construct a railroad track from the limestone quarry in Oatmanville, Texas to the capitol site to move the material.

The track was completed in March of 1884 and the first sixty tons of limestone were delivered to Austin. These stones were of such low quality that the Capital Commissioners rejected them. The superintendent of construction also discovered that "the limestone was unstable in color and that exposure to the weather would cause dirty, rusty colored streaks to appear on the stones." [4]

The contractor suggested that the building be constructed of Indiana limestone, but the Governor and legislature wanted to use only Texas materials. Negotiations on the use of red granite, quarried in Texas, brought work on the building to a standstill. This work stoppage

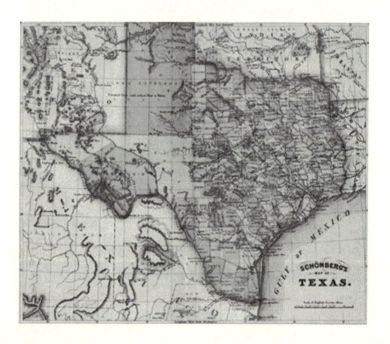

continued into July 1885. Finally, the contractor made a proposal that was accepted by the governor and the Capital Commissioners:

> I will construct the building, using Texas granite for the exterior wall; provided the state will furnish me a granite quarry accessible and suitable for the building, free of costs, and furnish such number of convicts as I may require, not to exceed 1000, I to board, clothe and guard them. The enclosed plan of construction for the exterior walls to be adopted, all the work to be rock faced. The three porticoes to be eliminated. Such alterations and changes to be made to the interior work as will conform to this plan, not detrimental to the building, and to lessen the cost at least $100,000. The time for the completion of the building to be extended three years. [5]

Work on the capitol was further delayed when organized labor strongly opposed the use of convict labor in the construction of a state building, declaring such use unfair competition.

Additional problems arose between the contractor and the International Association of Granite Cutters, causing the union to boycott the job.

Then the contractor imported granite cutters from Scotland. The International Association of Granite Cutters challenged this action and it was held to be a violation of the Alien Contract Labor Law, which was passed in February 1885. Charges were filed in the Federal District Court at Austin, and the syndicate was found to be in violation of the law.

The fine imposed was $1,000 for each of the imported stone workers, for a total of $64,000, but the contractor appealed to Washington and four years later, the fine was reduced to $8,000 and costs. The building was completed on December 8, 1888, nearly seven years after the contract was let. [6]

At the time it was completed, the Texas state house was the second largest building in the United States. The red granite Capitol of Texas is still the largest state capitol building in the United States. [7]

Development of the XIT Ranch began well before the capitol building was completed. A. C. "Colonel" Babcock led a party of surveyors and cowboys to inspect the land in the spring of 1882. The northwest corner of the ranch was to match the northwest corner of the state as it had been established by the John H. Clark survey in 1859, lining up with the thirty-second parallel at its intersection with the 103rd meridian.

Babcock found discrepancies in records locating the northwest corner that left a strip approximately two and one-half miles wide and 310 miles long following the length of the Texas border to be claimed by the New Mexico territory. Congress finally settled ownership of

this strip by awarding it to Texas (and the XIT) when New Mexico became a state in 1912.

The XIT lands covered large parts of ten Texas Counties. They are Dallam, at the Oklahoma border, Hartley, Oldham, Deaf Smith, Parmer, Castro, Bailey, Lamb, Hockley, and a tiny sliver of Cochran County. There is discussion among historians as to the origin of the name XIT, but the number of counties clearly provided the name of the ranch.

The XIT brand (Ten in Texas) was said by some to be designed by a trail driver named Abner Blocker. In payment, Blocker was given the honor of placing the brand on the first cow released to graze on ranch property. [8] (Map-Appendix B)

Farwell, Babcock, and Taylor began the XIT with long term plans although the men were all more than sixty years old. They expected to operate a ranch only until the Panhandle was settled enough that they could profitably subdivide and sell their land. Railroad building in the Panhandle was encouraging the growth of commerce and settlement.

The thousands of immigrants who poured into west Texas in the years following the Civil War continued to move into the area. Dramatically increased land values seemed inevitable. Innovations in technology, including windmills to bring water to the surface of the prairie from deep wells and barbed wire fencing to protect herds and facilitate controlled stockbreeding also promised ever-growing profits from ranching.

In 1881 the "cattle bonanza" was at its height. After his survey of the property, Colonel Babcock encouraged the syndicate to join the boom and make as much money as possible from ranching while waiting for enough population growth and transportation facilities in the area to make subdividing and selling the land profitable.

Babcock's report to the owners estimated that 150,000 head of cattle purchased at the prevailing price of $20.00 per head would yield a ninety percent calf crop each year and a profit of more than thirty percent annually. He made no allowances however, for the natural hazards of unusually bitter winters, drought or other disasters that could be expected to endanger herds on a ranch that averaged twenty-seven miles wide and almost 200 miles long.

Neither Babcock nor members of the syndicate acknowledged the possibility of a decline in the market value of beef when the

A one-picture history of the XIT — space, a windmill, a pond of water and changing breeds of beef cattle.

tremendous increase in numbers of cattle created by the ranching craze reached market. He urged Farwell, Babcock, and Taylor to "place cattle and sheep on our lands--fence our lands in ranches. The cost of wire fence, when enclosing large tracts I ascertained to be less than ten cents an acre." [9]

Fencing and stocking a ranch of three million acres necessitated an investment of approximately two million dollars. In addition, constructing the minimum offices, bunkhouses, corrals and other needed buildings, plus digging wells and furnishing equipment to provide water required a much larger cash outlay than the syndicate had available.

To raise the needed money, The Capitol Company, as the syndicate was known, found it necessary to go to England, where interest in investing in the American cattle industry was still active. In London Farwell, Babcock, and Taylor created the Capitol Freehold Land and Investment Company, Limited. This company raised enough money through the sale of bonds to English investors to stock the ranch with a herd of 110,000 Spanish cattle from the Nueces

Valley area in Southern Texas during 1885/1886. [10]

The capital raised in England to develop the ranch led many to adopt the mistaken belief that the XIT was owned and operated by an English organization. Many of the ranches created during the boom were owned and operated by English investors, but the purchasers of the bonds issued by the Capitol Freehold Land and Investment Company did not own any part of the ranch. They simply owned the bonds of the holding company. When the bonds were completely redeemed in 1909, the English company was closed. A real estate trust named the Capitol Reservation Lands was formed in 1909 to manage the subdivision and sale of the lands then remaining.[11]

In 1886, it's first full year of operation, the XIT built 781 miles of fence. Each year thereafter the amount increased until approximately 6000 miles of four-strand barbed wire fencing kept the cattle on the home range. By 1900 the ranch consisted of ninety-four pastures, separated by fences, each devoted to a particular purpose.

Mexican laborers cut Cedar poles for fence posts in the brakes along the Canadian River. This was the only timber available on most of the range. Barbed wire was shipped from Chicago by railroad and unloaded at El Moro, a station near Trinidad, Colorado. From there freighters loaded the wire on two-horse wagons and delivered it to the ranch as part of their contract, they "placed four spools of wire every quarter of a mile along the fence line."

Poles were placed thirty feet apart, and attaching one of the spools to a wagon and pulling the wire taut stretched the wire. Once the wire was in place, it was attached to the poles by heavy staples. Fencing the XIT used three hundred railroad carloads of barbed wire, over "100,000 posts, five carloads of wire staves, and one car of staples." So many gates were required "the general manager just ordered a carload of gate hinges." [12]

The first ranch buildings were constructed at Buffalo Springs. These buildings served as headquarters for the ranching operation north of the Canadian River.

In time the ranch was cut into seven divisions, each of which was handled from separate headquarters. The ranch houses were well improved residences, and cellars, bunkhouses, storerooms, barns and corrals were built at each location. Eventually the XIT came to be known as one of the best-equipped and most systematically arranged ranches in the country. [13]

In 1886 a few buildings were erected at Yellow Houses to serve the southern ranges, but the cost of freighting supplies, groceries, windmills, and building materials 150 miles over rough trails from Colorado City on the Texas and Pacific Railroad delayed the work and drastically increased the cost.

The Fort Worth and Denver Railroad was completed into the Panhandle in 1887, and the XIT built a warehouse in Tascosa. After that, the ranch purchased all supplies in wholesale lots. Salt and many other necessities were ordered by the carload. [14]

In 1890 the syndicate moved its general headquarters to the town of Channing on the

Canadian River. Buffalo Springs, Middle Water, Rito Blanco, and Ojo Bravo, all north of the Canadian served as secondary headquarters. Individual pastures were given such names as Farwell Park, Matlock, and Carrizo.

To the South, Spring Lake, Yellow Houses, Escarbada and Amarillo provided local management and service sites. When the Pecos Valley and Southern Railroad (locally known as

the Pea Vine) was completed, a new warehouse was built at Bovina to supply the southern ranches. [15]

In addition to managers at each headquarters and a general manager, bookkeepers and a few miscellaneous laborers, approximately one hundred and fifty cowboys worked on the ranch. In addition, fencing crews, equipped with a wagon carrying supplies patrolled the fences. Windmillers moved from

well to well, maintaining and repairing the windmills. Oversight of the entire operation was direct from Chicago.

The syndicate created and distributed strict rules for the cowboy's and other ranch workers conduct, many dictated by the demands of the huge operation. No gambling or drinking of alcoholic beverages was allowed. Neither pistols nor other hand weapons were permitted. When not at headquarters the cowboys rode about their work accompanied by a chuck wagon and made camp each night near the herds. A copy of the ranch rules was posted prominently at each camp. (Appendix A)

The chuck wagons carried supplies to provide meals of surprising variety. Trail logs reveal purchases of flour, bacon, baking powder, coffee, oatmeal, and spices. Every grocery order included dried fruit. They ordered raisins, prunes, apples, and currants in amounts that indicate they were eaten every day. At least seventy pounds of potatoes were bought at one time. Dried beans were a diet staple. In addition to the fruit and vegetables, beef was supplied from the herds, although under strict regulations. Records indicate the company furnished their employees chewing and smoking tobacco.[16]

The rules stated that cowboys were not permitted to keep their own workhorses on the ranch, but could pasture pleasure-riding horses.

The employment rules included immediate dismissal for abusing a horse or mule by striking it on its head, spurring it harshly or for any neglect. [17]

Prairie fires and rustlers were always a menace on the range. Employee regulation charged that each cowboy must attempt to extinguish any fire on pain of dismissal. Strangers were watched carefully, and rules allowed travelers and strangers to remain in camp for one night only, paying for the care of their horses and their own food. Freighters delivering on the ranch were not invited to eat in camp, but required to carry their own food supplies and feed for their livestock. [18]

The XIT owned and worked thousands of horses and mules. They maintained cattle herds totaling 150,000 from about 1885, until the ranch was faced with receivership in 1901 and was forced to reduce its holdings. Beginning with scrub cattle descended from Spanish stock, the syndicate first introduced the Aberdeen Angus, hoping to create a breed with more meat on its bones, but the cross that resulted was not hardy.

When Herefords and Shorthorns were crossed with the Spanish cattle however, the result proved to be satisfactory. They gradually created a breed with more meat on its hindquarters and promised to be much more profitable. The new crossbred cattle were hardy. Like the Spanish cattle, they could survive on the range winter and summer. [19]

The Panhandle was ideally suited to cattle raising. Natural grasses covered the area. They were mainly grama, buffalo, and mesquite. These grasses furnished excellent, highly nutritious grazing all summer long. They also cured naturally to provide hay for winter feed where they grew, without the necessity of cutting, gathering, or storage. Scrub cattle from south Texas and the crossbreeds created by breeding them with Herefords, and Shorthorns survived and increased in weight when fed on these grasses, requiring no additional feed, even during the harsh winters. [20]

The XIT, like many other Texas ranches, maintained finishing ranges in Montana and the Dakotas. "It was common knowledge to the cow country that steers matured in the north spread in loin and frame and grew to greater size." A herd of ten to fifteen thousand steers each year walked more than one thousand miles up the Northern Trail to range between the Yellowstone and the Missouri rivers. Here they were fattened for two years then were shipped by rail to the heavy-beef markets in Chicago. When the trails were closed to Texas cattle during the 1890s during the "tick fever" scare the XIT continued to move cattle to finishing pastures by rail. [21]

The first stock purchased by the XIT was pastured in the well-watered Buffalo Springs country. The southern half of the range however, was sadly short of water. Before large numbers of cattle could be placed on that range a solution had to be found. The syndicate hired a well drilling company to sink several wells and have them completed and in operation before the herds arrived.

The well drilling was at first a great disappointment. Only two holes yielded water, and the flow was too slow to satisfy thousands of cattle. In some areas of that country the water table was only twelve to fifteen feet below the surface and many shallow wells were dug by hand and outfitted with horse-driven pumps.

Small dams were built across arroyos to catch the run-off from heavy rains. Shallow wells were later fitted with windmills. The windmills used were on a frame thirty to thirty-five feet tall and their wheels measured twelve to eighteen feet across. They pumped water into raised cypress tubs, and it poured down wooden chutes into earthen tanks. "By 1900 there were three hundred thirty-five windmills and one hundred dams on the ranch, estimated to have cost one-half million dollars." [22]

Herds of cattle totaling 15,000 head were under contract to be delivered to the southern range in the spring of 1887. The wells were not finished when the cattle began to arrive. The last drive to the headquarters near Yellow Houses covered sixty miles without water. The herds arrived frantic with thirst. Dozens of cattle died for lack of water, but by pumping water from the wells with horse pumps and by hand, most of the herd was saved. The shortage of water made the cattle unruly and worked the cowboys and their horses to exhaustion. [23]

Colonel A. G. Boyce, an experienced cattleman, was put in charge of the ranch at that time.? He immediately took charge and moved the herds to water. On the morning of the 27th, I prevailed on Stuart, who was in charge Of the "Q" herd, to let me have part of his horses, and these I turned over to Ney, and told him to take them and what men he could spare, and gather all the cattle, and drift them north to Sod Houses,and there water all the cattle he could, leaving such as he considered too weak to travel, and taking the balance on to Spring Lake. [24]

Additional cowboys were always hired for the roundup, and Bill Derrick came to the XIT as an "extra" hand for spring roundup. He describes one of the methods used by the XIT foremen to find the extra men needed:

In the spring of 1904, I was on the Santa Fe train and had my Saddle with me in an old coffee-sack in the baggage coach. When the train stopped at Bovina, Texas, C. R. Smith, the foreman of the XIT came aboard looking for hands to make up the roundup crew. They always hired extra hands in the summer months, but kept only the regular cowboys in the winter.

I hired out on the train and after getting my saddle loaded in the spring wagon, Mr. Smith and I started for the Escarbada headquarters, a sub-division of the XIT. After the roundup was over that summer, I was sent to the Tierra Blanca Camp on the east line. That was mainly a fence riding job. I would go north one day and stay all night at Tombstone Camp and ride back the next. Then to the corner south and then west. I'd meet the other fence riders at Friona and return to Tierra Blanca Camp the next day.

They had telephones in all camps even in those days. The lines came out from Hereford and went around the ranch on the barbed wire fence; all were connected to headquarters. It was a wonderful thing for an outfit of that size and saved many a long ride. [25]

The XIT cattle operation was slow to make a profit, and when it did, the returns were so small they did not satisfy the company's English investors. From early in 1901, the land was gradually sold. At first large sections of land were sold at wholesale prices. The syndicate wanted to quickly obtain enough cash to buy out the English investors.

From 1902 until 1912, the herds were gradually reduced and land continued to be sold until the company was no longer in the cattle business. From 1912 until 1950, when more than 100,000 people lived on the three million acres that originally made up the XIT, the syndicate devoted itself exclusively to colonization and land sales.[26]

The George G. Wright Land Company of Kansas City, Missouri contracted to sell one of the first large plots for the Capital Freehold Land and Investment Company. First it was necessary for them to establish a local base to host prospective land buyers. In Parmer County, a tract of land near Frio Draw, and adjacent to the Santa Fe Railroad tracks was surveyed into town lots and called Friona. The land company advertised widely and established agents in Ohio, Indiana, Illinois, Iowa, Missouri, Nebraska, and Kansas.[27]

On the first and third Wednesdays of each month "Land Excursion Trains" collected prospective buyers in Kansas City and delivered them in Friona the next day. Each train brought from 250 to 500 prospective settlers.? Land was offered in parcels of forty to one hundred and sixty acres.? Most buyers planned to build a home and convert the land from grassland to farming:

> In the early 1900s several land companies built hotels well outside key railroad stops to accommodate clients they brought in from the East or Midwest. One such hotel was constructed on the prairie near Bovina.
>
> Residents and business people would crowd around the depot when a train arrived carrying "landseekers," sometimes referred to by locals as "land suckers." The land men who had attracted the visitors tried hard to keep their clients from fraternizing with local people, who might utter discouraging words about the area or who might tell them about lower local real estate prices.

So fleets of automobiles or buggies would await the travelers at the depot, pick them up and take them to the remote hotels outside town, where the land men could give their spiels without fear of contradiction. [28]

Unusual and severe drought hit the Panhandle in 1908 and lasted for several years. Many of the farmer-settlers failed so miserably they abandoned or sold their land and left the area. The people who remained found growing cattle or sheep much safer and more profitable than trying to farm the semi-arid plains. Two years of drought were followed by a severe blizzard and prolonged cold spell, that in turn destroyed cattle and sheep.

Parmer County and Friona were typical of many areas of the plains. Settlers moved in and applied the farming methods they learned in well-watered land to the east and failed, returning the land to grazing. It was not until dry farming methods were greatly improved in the late 1930s that the area became prosperous through combined farming and ranching. [29]

Capitol Freehold Land and Investment Company continued to sell land, finally exhausting its holdings in the 1950s. The land once surrounded by six thousand miles of barbed wire fence is now criss-crossed by public roads, without gates, and dotted with towns.

The XIT was the largest ranch under

fence in the United States and probably the largest in the world. It was a product of the boom times in America in the 1880s and demonstrates the concurrent development of some of the modern management methods needed for success in large business operations. Telephones, windmills, pumps, and barbed wire, products of the nineteenth century flood of technological improvements, also played an important part in the establishment and operation of the XIT.

APPENDIX A:

General Rules of the XIT Ranch

COWBOYS AT ES CABADA BUNK HOUSE. X I T RANCH 1891

January 1888

No. 1: When a person is engaged to work on the ranch, the person so engaging him will fill out and sign a blank, giving the name of the party employed, for what purpose employed, and the amount of wages he is to receive, the date he will begin to work and deliver the same to the person employed, who must sign the counterpart of such contract, which must be forwarded to headquarters at the first opportunity; and no one will be put upon the Company's pay roll, or receive any pay until this is complied with.

No. 2: Employees, when discharged, or on leaving the Company's service, are required to bring or send to the headquarter office, a statement from the person under whom they were at work, showing the day they quit the company's service, and no settlement will be made with any employee, until such statement is furnished.

No. 3: Employees discharged from or leaving the service of the Company are expected to leave the ranch at once and will not be permitted to remain more than one night in any camp.

No. 4: The wages due any employee will not be paid to any other person without a written order from the employee to whom such wages are due.

No. 5: No person in charge of any pasture, or any work on the ranch, or any contractor on the ranch, will be permitted to hire anyone who had been discharged from the Company's service; nor shall anyone who leaves an outfit, of his own accord, with the intention of getting employment at some other place on the ranch, be so employed except by special agreement, made beforehand between the person in charge of the outfit he leaves and the one in charge of the outfit he wishes to work for.

No. 6: Private horses of employees must not be kept at any of the camps, nor will they be allowed to be fed grain belonging to the Company. No employee shall be permitted to keep more than two private horses on the ranch and all such horses must be kept in some pasture designated by the ranch manager.

No. 7: No employee shall be permitted to own any cattle or stock horses on the ranch.

No. 8: The killing of beef by any person on the ranch, except by the person in charge of the pasture, or under his instruction, is strictly forbidden. Nor is any person in charge of a pasture allowed to have beef killed, unless it can be distributed and consumed without lass. And all hides of beef killed must be taken care of and accounted for. It shall be the duty of each person having beef killed to keep a tally of the same and report the number, age, and sex killed to headquarters every month.

No. 9: The abuse of horses, mules, or cattle by any employee will not be tolerated; and anyone who strikes his horse or mule over the head, or spurs it in the shoulder, or in any other manner abuses or neglects to care for it while in his charge, shall be dismissed from the Company's service.

No. 10: Employees are not allowed to run mustang, antelope, or any kind of game on the Company's horses.

No. 11: No Employee of the Company, or any contractor doing work for the Company, is permitted to carry on or about his person or in his saddle bags, any pistol, dirk, dagger, sling shot, knuckles, bowie knife or any other similar instruments for the purpose of offense or defense. Guests of the Company, and persons not employees of the ranch temporarily staying at any of its camps, are expected to comply with this rule, which is also a State law.

No. 12: Card playing and gambling of every description, whether engaged in by employees, or by persons not in service of the Company is strictly forbidden on the ranch.

No. 13: In case of fire upon the ranch, or on lands bordering on the same, it shall be the duty of every employee to go to it at once and use his best endeavors to extinguish it, and any neglect to do so, without reasonable excuse, will be considered sufficient cause for dismissal.

No. 14: Each outfit of men that is furnished with a wagon and cook is required to make its own camping places, and not impose on the other camps on the ranch unnecessarily.

No. 15: Employees are strictly forbidden the use of vinous, malt, spirituous, or intoxicating liquors, during their time of service with the Company.

No. 16: It is the duty of every employee to protect the Company's interests to the best of his ability, and when he sees they are threatened in any direction to take every proper measure at his command to accomplish this end, and as soon as possible to inform his employers of the danger threatened.

No. 17: Employees of neighboring ranches on business are to be cared for at all camps, and their horses fed if desired (provided there is feed in the camp to spare); but such persons will not be expected to remain on the ranch longer than is necessary to transact their business, or continue their journey.

No. 18: Bona fide travelers may be sheltered if convenient, but they will be expected to pay for what grain and provisions they get, at prices to be fixed from time to time by the Company, and all such persons must not remain at any camp longer than one night.

No. 19: Persons not in the employment of the Company, but freighting for it, are not to be furnished with meals for themselves or feed for their teams at any of the camps on the ranch, but are expected to come on the ranch prepared to take care of themselves.

No. 20: Loafers, "sweaters," deadbeats, tramps, gamblers, or disreputable persons, must not be entertained at any camp, nor will employees be permitted to give, loan or sell such persons any grain, or provisions of any kind, nor shall such persons be permitted to remain on the Company's land anywhere under any pretext whatever.

No. 21: No person or persons, not in the employment of the Company, shall be permitted to hunt or kill game of any kind, inside of the ranch enclosure, under any pretext whatever, and all employees are instructed to see that this rule is enforced. Employees of the Company will also not be permitted to hunt or kill game except when necessary for use for food.

No. 22: It is the aim of the owners of this ranch to conduct it on the principle of right and justice to everyone: and for it to be excelled by no other in the good behavior, sterling honesty and integrity, and general high character of its employees, and to this end it is necessary that the forgoing rules be adhered to, and the violation of any of them will be considered just charge for discharge.

No. 23: Every camp will be furnished with a printed copy of these rules, which must be nailed up in a conspicuous place in the camp; and each and every rule is hereby made and considered a condition and part of the engagement between the Company and its employees, and any employee who shall tear down or destroy such printed rules, or shall cause the same to be done, shall be discharged.

By order of the Company,
Amos Taylor, Manager [30]

Appendix: B XIT COUNTRY[31]

End Notes

[1] Texas Legislative Council, Capitol, p 31.

[2] Texas Legislative Council, Capitol, p 32.

[3] Haley, The XIT p 55.

[4] Texas Legislative Council, Capitol, p 42.

[5] Texas Legislative Council, Capitol, p 42.

[6] Texas Legislative Council, Capitol, pp 42-44.

[7] Fort Worth Telegram, Sunday, January 13, 1963.

Section One, Page 4

[8] Haley, The XIT, pp 64-65; Lewis, Horace Nelson, A History of Parmer County Texas, Quanah, Texas, Nortex Press, pp 23-27.

[9] Haley, The XIT, pp 70-71.

[10] Crodia Sloan Duke and Joe B. Frantz, 6,000 Miles of Fence: Life on the XIT Ranch of Texas, 1972, Austin, Texas, University of Texas Press, p 7.

[11] Taylor to A.C. Babcock, March 20 and April 21, 1883, and Taylor to Farwell, July, 1883. (taken from the abstract of a deed to lot 27, Friona Acres, Parmer County Texas, owned by H. Nelson Lewis, Landrum, South Carolina).

[12] Haley, The XIT, p 88; Duke and Franz, 6,000 Miles of Fence, pp 5-7.

[13] Haley, The XIT, p 97.

[14] Haley, The XIT, p 9.

[15] The Amarillo Daily News, "Brand of XIT," Monday, November 13, 1995, p 1C; Lewis, H. Nelson, A History of Parmer County, p 22.

[16] Duke and Frantz, 6,000 Miles of Fence, pp 170-172.

[17] (See rules), Appendix A.

[18] Haley, The XIT, pp 241-245.

[19] Duke and Frantz, 6,000 Miles of Fence, p 6.

[20] Haley, The XIT, p 69.

[21] Haley, The XIT, pp 125-143.

[22] Haley, The XIT, p 96.

[23] Haley, The XIT, pp 96-98.

[24]Haley, The XIT, p 92, (from letter; Boyce to George Findlay, December 3, 1888, Matlock Papers).

[25] Lewis, Parmer County Texas, Volume 1, pp 30-33, by Bill Derrick as told to Harvey Lafon, from True West, May-June, 1965.

[26]J. Evetts Haley, Southwestern Reporter, Volume 65, p 510, (lawsuit filed by Mrs. Amos C. Babcock and Morris K. Brown against the Farwells and the Capitol Freehold Land and Investment Company, Limited, on behalf of all the minor stockholders charging that the Farwells were using the ranch for the of their interests to the detriment of the minority stockholders); Duke and Frantz, 6000 Miles of Fence,

[27]Lewis, H. Nelson, Parmer County Texas, Volume 1, p 28.

[28] Robertson, Pauline Durrett, and R. L. Robertson, 1989, quoted in The Amarillo Daily News, Monday, November 13, 1995, p 1C.

[29]Works Projects Administration, O.P. No. 65-6-3-299 (report on Parmer County), pp 80-81.
Promotion

[30]Haley, The XIT, (Appendix A), pp 241-245.

[31]Duke and Frantz, 6000 Miles of Fence, (Appendix B, XIT Country Map), p 13.

Chapter One of Ten In Texas
ISBN-10: 1530756588
ISBN-13: 978-1530756582
ASIN- B01EDDUA7W

Will Gantry walked his horse down the middle of the broad, dirt street. On his left he saw a hardware store, a lumberyard, and a livery stable. All three seemed to be doing a thriving business. Across the way, a two-story, barracks-like hotel appeared a beehive of activity. The building sat halfway up the hill from the railroad, its two-story bulk towering over the rest of the town.

Below the hotel and only a few hundred feet from the railroad, a new bungalow sat in the midst of a well-tended plot. Fruit trees, a kitchen garden and bright green sprigs of Rose of Sharon, newly planted but thriving nicely, surrounded the attractive place.

A semicircle of large touring cars, tops folded rakishly back, sat close to the brand-new railroad station which gleamed in fresh yellow paint. Bold, black letters across the gable end announced the travelers' arrival in Friona, Texas.

Three passenger cars, a baggage car, and a dozen freight cars shunted onto the siding next to the new station. A crowd of people stood in the bright sunshine, silent, listening to the words of a nattily dressed man. Will edged his horse closer so he could hear the speaker's words.

The salesman delivered a spiel polished by repetition.

"Land is available in any direction, folks. You'll find that prices are ridiculously low, the terms are within reach of anyone. All the area is virgin prairie, deep in top soil without the hazards of rocks, gullies, swamps, tree stumps or noxious weeds."

The speaker, for all his eloquence, failed to mention the land also lacked sufficient rainfall to sustain farm crops. Finally, the man waved toward the line of waiting horseless carriages.

A wild rush for the automobiles followed his last remarks. Men clambered for seats as drivers bent to crank the motors to start the cars. Amid the roar of exhausts and swirls of dust, the loaded cars left the station yard. The majority turned either northwest or southeast, traveling over barely discernable paths.

Those men who didn't take part in the general exodus from the Friona station gathered in small groups around the fast-talking land agents. As the sounds of the loaded cars died away, the knots of men separated to drift toward the hotel, the hardware store, and the lumber yard.

With a gentle pull on the reins, Will turned his horse to face the east. He watched with avid interest the activity around the box cars, as the big doors slid back to reveal farm machinery, household goods, and livestock.

Men and boys labored to roll farm wagons down plank ramps and guide them to the edge of the hard-packed dirt beside the tracks. Horses and mules, ears pointed forward, their legs still shaky from the jolting of the long train ride, picked their way down the rough board ramp.

The cold, clear water in the long wooden trough refreshed them. Familiar hands led them to be hitched to their own wagons. It took a lot of time to fit all the tools and implements into the wagons.

When it was time to load a wagon designated to haul household furniture, the ladies in the crowd came alive. Suggestions, demands, cries, even screams of caution rang out.

"That barrel has all my good dishes in it."

"Don't drop that box. It's full of canned goods."

"Careful. You scratched Great-Grandma's bed."

Despite all the hard work and anxiety of the unloading and reloading, Will sensed a holiday attitude among the settlers and a pioneer spirit. Each family seemed to know that somewhere out on the broad prairie, a tiny speck of land a place to build a home waited for them.

Poor dreamin' fools.

There's no question about it. Few of these families will stay and really prosper. Many will put forth a half-hearted effort, then quickly give in to the ravages of drought, loneliness, and the oppression of poverty. A small percentage are no more than opportunists looking for a gold-brick type of living that could never exist on the high plains of Texas.

The more serious-minded settlers among the group foresaw the hazards of climate and the difficulties of wresting a living, much less a fortune, from the unbroken sod. These families probably spent days discussing the possibilities of bettering their lot in the newly-opened lands. They expected what they already knew, nothing but hard work and privation.

Many risks were considered. Heads of families came ahead on excursion trains, their fares paid by a land company from Chicago or other cities, to inspect the plains country. For the most part, they liked what they saw.

Upon their return home, they extolled the virtues of Texas.

Friends, family and neighbors met their glowing reports with true and imagined arguments against taking the risks. Did not wild Indians roam all of Texas, they asked? Would they find churches, schools, and hospitals?

Some believed repossession of Texas by Mexico was still a possibility. Others asked, what kind of state is it that has to trade barren, God-forsaken land in order to build a capitol building? If Texas is so great, why isn't it organized as New York City or even Milledgeville, Georgia are?

Horny-handed farmers listened patiently. Wives, in-laws and neighbors argued and influenced many ambitious men to stay in the supposedly secure environment of the well-settled eastern or mid-western states. Others, the more determined ones, sold their farms to anxious neighbors and chartered box cars for the move to Texas.

The black horse stamped an impatient hoof.

Be still. Will spoke, as if to a person. He continued to watch the heavily-laden wagons leave the depot yard, their human cargoes chattering and bright-eyed with excitement.

The sun moved almost straight overhead

before he turned to ride back up the main street. A large new building, also painted yellow, a block to the west, caught his eye. Tall black letters painted on the bright wall announced, "Boarding House."

Tying Apache at the hitch rack, Will entered the crowded dining room. The meal was being served "family style." In boarding houses, that's another way of saying, "We put the food on the table you catch as catch can."

Large china bowls of vegetables and platters of fried meat ranged down the middle of the table. Plates of hot biscuits passed from hand to hand and seldom completed even one round of the hungry diners.

Will found an empty chair and heaped his plate with the steaming vegetables. Meat was no problem on the trail, but fresh garden truck took too long to cook at a campfire. A huge platter stacked high with squares of golden cornbread was another welcome sight. He settled down to business and did full justice to his first home-cooked meal in months.

He didn't join in the bits of conversation he heard between the clatter of dishes and the slurping of coffee. "This-here stranger, he walks up to me and he says, 'Friend, what is your main money crop around here?'

The speaker looked and sounded an old timer. Suckers, I told him. The old man's story got a few chuckles and few hard looks from younger men dressed as land agents.

"For heaven's sake no, absolutely not. Don't go to Findley, there ain't no water out there," someone said. The remark proved to contain more truth than poetry. "I'd go south or southeast. There's water, grass, and the best land thataway."

Another speaker leaned toward his prospective customer. "Don't go too far south. There's a big ravine down there where a wild Indian couldn't raise a ruckus with a full pint of whiskey."

As a newcomer to the table, Will just listened. He noticed a group of big, broad-shouldered men with blond hair at the end of the table. They also remained quiet. When either of the men spoke, he spoke to a member of his own crowd. Their voices and arrangement of English words carried a distinct Germanic flavor.

Almost finished, Will looked around the table--how plainly these men wore their labels. The serious minded farmers, the flashily dressed salesmen, and the cold-eyed businessmen, most of them speculators, buying large tracts of land for profitable resale. These were men who never intended to spend even one night on the prairie.

Placing a coin on the table, Will got up and left. A quick glance around the town's empty streets proved the inner man wants satisfaction three times a day. The crowds were inside, eating. He smiled sardonically as he untied his horses' reins and climbed into the saddle. He remembered weeks without three square meals.

"Let's go, Apache." He turned the horse south toward the railroad.

Where the main street met the east-west road, an eager-voiced young salesman stepped out in front of his horse and looked up at Will. "Are you a landseeker?" he asked.

"Sure am. I'm A. Plowman, at your service, and what's your name? Will leaned toward the man without-stretched hand.

"Aw, forget it." Scowling at Will's humor, the young man retreated, waving Will away.

Come on, Apache." Will galloped west out of Friona along the dirt road beside the railroad tracks to check out the town of Bovina.

Anne Haw Holt

Anne Haw Holt, writing as A. H. Holt, is a Virginian transplanted to a 1910 Cracker cottage in Monticello, Florida. She attended PVCC in Charlottesville, Va. and received her BA from Mary Baldwin in Staunton, VA in 1989. She holds a MA and Ph.D. in History from Florida State University in Tallahassee, Florida.

Anne is an accomplished storyteller and photographer. She writes fiction, poetry, and non-fiction on writing, history, parenting and Frontier Florida. Dr. Holt writes grants and teaches writing, grant writing, and leadership.

Other Books By A. H. Holt

Fiction

High Plains Fort
Ten in Texas
Silver Creek
Blanco Sol
Riding Fence
Kendrick
Blood Redemption

Nonfiction

Grant Writing Step by Step
From Writer to Author
Beautiful Places:
Monticello & Jefferson County Florida

Thank you for reading this book.
Please take the time to share
and leave a review.

Made in the USA
Columbia, SC
08 March 2025